Crossing
the River

ISBN # 1-57873-063-5

JZK Publishing
Ramtha's School of Enlightenment
A Division of JZK, Inc.

P.O. Box 1210
Yelm, Washington 98597
360.458.5201
800.347.0439
www.ramtha.com
www.jzkpublishing.com

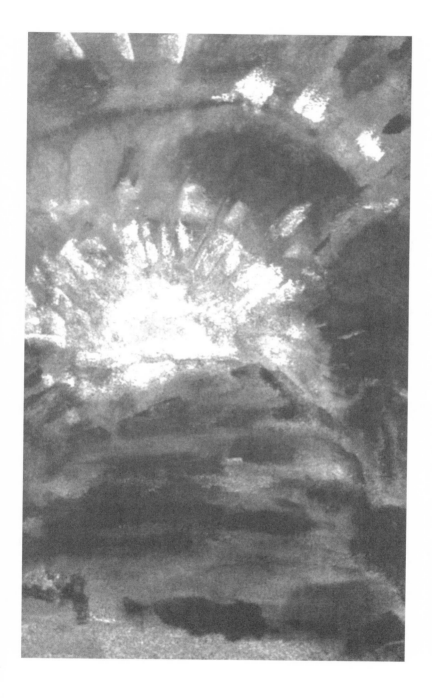

These series of teachings are designed for all the students of the Great Work who love the teachings of the Ram.

It is suggested that you create an ideal learning environment for study and contemplation.

Light your fireplace and get cozy. Prepare yourself. Open your mind to learn and be genius.

FOREWORD

The Fireside Series Collection Library is an ongoing library of the hottest topics of interest taught by Ramtha. These series of teachings are designed for all the students of the Great Work who love the teachings of the Ram. This library collection is also intended as a continuing learning tool for the students of Ramtha's School of Enlightenment and for everyone interested and familiar with Ramtha's teachings. In the last three decades Ramtha has continuously and methodically deepened and expanded his exposition of the nature of reality and its practical application through various disciplines. It is assumed by the publisher that the reader has attended a Beginning Retreat or workshop through Ramtha's School of Enlightenment or is at least familiar with Ramtha's instruction to his beginning class of students. This required information for beginning students is found in *Ramtha: A Beginner's Guide to Creating Reality*, Third Ed. (Yelm: JZK Publishing, a division of JZK, Inc., 2004).

We have included in the Fireside Series a glossary of some of the basic concepts used by Ramtha so the reader can become familiarized with these teachings. We have also included a brief introduction of Ramtha by JZ Knight that describes how all this began. Enjoy your learning and contemplation.

Contents

Introduction by JZ Knight:
How It All Started

"In other words, his whole point of focus is to come here and to teach you to be extraordinary."

My name is JZ Knight and I am the rightful owner of this body. Ramtha and I are two different people, two different beings. We have a common reality point and that is usually my body. Though we sort of look the same, we really don't look the same.

All of my life, ever since I was a little person, I have heard voices in my head and I have seen wonderful things that to me in my life were normal. I was fortunate enough to have a mother who was a very psychic human being and never condemned what it was that I was seeing. I had wonderful experiences all my life but the most important experience was that I had this deep and profound love for God and there was a part of me that understood what that was. Later in my life I went to church and I tried to understand God from the viewpoint of religious doctrine and had a lot of difficulty with that because it was sort of in conflict with what I felt and what I knew.

Ramtha has been a part of my life ever since I was born, but I didn't know who he was and I didn't know what he was, only that there was a wonderful force that walked with me, and when I was in trouble — and I had a lot of pain in my life growing up — that I always had extraordinary experiences with this being who would talk to me. I could hear him as clearly as I can hear you if we were to have a conversation. He helped me to understand a lot of things in my life that were beyond the normal scope of what someone would give someone as advice.

It wasn't until 1977 that he appeared to me in my kitchen on a Sunday afternoon as I was making pyramids with my husband. We were dehydrating food because we were into hiking and backpacking. As I put one of these ridiculous things on my head, at the other end of my kitchen this wonderful apparition appeared that was seven feet tall and glittery and beautiful and stark. You just don't expect at 2:30 in the afternoon that this is going to appear in your kitchen. No one is ever prepared for that. So Ramtha at that time really made his appearance known to me.

The first thing I said to him — and I don't know where this came from — was, "You are so beautiful. Who are you?" He has a smile like the sun. He is extraordinarily handsome. He said, "My name is Ramtha the Enlightened One and I have come to help you over the ditch." Being the simple person that I am, my immediate reaction was to look at the floor because I thought maybe something had happened to the floor, or the bomb was being dropped. I didn't know. From that day forward he became a constant in my life. And during the year of 1977 a lot of interesting things happened, to say the least. My two younger children at that time got to meet Ramtha and got to experience some incredible phenomena, as well as my husband.

Later that year, after teaching me and having some difficulty telling me what he was and me understanding, one day he said to me, "I am going to send you a runner that will bring you a set of books, and you read them because then you will know what I am." Those books were called the *Life and Teaching of the Masters of the Far East* (DeVorss & Co. Publishers, 1964). I read them and I began to understand that Ramtha was one of those beings, in a way, and that took me out of the are-you-the-devil-or-are-you-God sort of category that was plaguing me at the time.

After I got to understand him he spent long, long moments walking into my living room, all seven feet of this beautiful being, making himself comfortable on my couch, sitting down and talking to me and teaching me. What I didn't realize at that particular time was he already knew all the things I was going to ask and he already knew how to answer them, but I didn't know that he knew that.

Since 1977 he patiently dealt with me in a manner that allowed me to question not his authenticity but things about myself as God, teaching me, catching me when I would get caught up in dogma or get caught up in limitation, catching me just in time and teaching me and walking me through that. And I always said, "You know, you are so patient. I think it is wonderful that you are so patient." And he would just smile and say that he is 35,000 years old, what else can you do in that period of time? It wasn't until about ten years ago that I realized that he already knew what I was going to ask and that is why he was so patient. But as the grand teacher that he is, he allowed me the opportunity to address these issues in myself. He had the grace to speak to me in a way that was not presumptuous but, as a true teacher, would allow me to come to realizations on my own.

Channeling Ramtha since late 1979 has been an experience. Ram is seven feet tall and he wears two robes that I have always seen him in. Even though they are the same robe, they are really beautiful so you never get tired of seeing them. The inner robe is snow white and goes all the way down to where I presume his feet are, and then he has an overrobe that is beautiful purple. You should understand that I have really looked at the material on these robes and it is not really material; it is sort of like light. And though the light has a transparency to them, there is an understanding that what he is wearing has a reality to it.

Ramtha's face is cinnamon-colored skin, and that is the best way I can describe it. It is not really brown and it is not really white and it is not really red. It is sort of a blending of that. He has very deep black eyes that can look into you, and you know you are being looked into. He has eyebrows that look like wings of a bird that come high on his brow. He has a very square jaw and a beautiful mouth, and when he smiles you know that you are in heaven. He has long, long hands and long fingers that he uses very eloquently to demonstrate his thought.

Imagine then after he taught me to get out of my body by actually pulling me out, throwing me in the tunnel, hitting the wall of light and bouncing back — and realizing my kids were home from school and I just got through doing breakfast dishes — that getting used to missing time on this plane was really difficult. I didn't understand what I was doing and where I was going, so we had a lot of practice sessions. You have to understand that he did this to me at ten o'clock in the morning and when I came back off of the white wall it was 4:30. I had a real problem trying to adjust with the time that was missing here. So we had a long time with Ramtha teaching me how to do that, and it was fun and frolic and absolutely terrifying at moments. You can imagine if he walked up to you, yanked you right out of your body, threw you up to the ceiling and said, "Now what does that view look like?" and then throwing you in a tunnel — and perhaps the best way to describe it is it is a black hole into the next level — and being flung through this tunnel and hitting this white wall and having amnesia.

What he was getting me ready to do was to teach me something that I had already agreed to prior to this incarnation. My destiny in this life was not just to marry and to have children and to do well in life but to overcome the adversity to let what was previously planned happen, and that happening included an extraordinary consciousness, which he is.

Trying to dress my body for Ramtha was a joke. I didn't know what to do. The first time we had a channeling session I wore heels and a skirt. I thought I was going to church. So you can imagine, if you have a little time to study him, how he would appear dressed up in a business suit with heels on, which he never walked in in his life.

It is really difficult to talk to people and have them

understand that I am not him, that we are two separate beings and that when you talk to me in this body, you are talking to me and not him. Sometimes over the past decade or so, that has been a great challenge to me in the public media because people don't understand how it is possible that a human being can be endowed with a divine mind and yet be separate from it.

I wanted you to know that although you see Ramtha out here in my body, it is my body, but he doesn't look anything like this. His appearance in the body doesn't lessen the magnitude of who and what he is. You should also know that when we do talk, when you start asking me about things that he said, I may not have a clue what you are talking about because when I leave my body, I am gone to a whole other time and another place that I don't have cognizant memory of. And however long he spends with you, to me that will be maybe about five minutes or three minutes. And when I come back to my body, this whole time of this whole day has passed and I wasn't a part of it. I didn't hear what he said to you and I don't know what he did out here. When I come back, my body is exhausted. It is hard to get up the stairs sometimes to change my clothes and make myself more presentable for what the day is bringing me, or what is left of the day.

He has shown me a lot of wonderful things that I suppose people who have never gotten to see couldn't even dream of in their wildest dreams. I have seen the twenty-third universe and I have met extraordinary beings and I have seen life come and go. I have watched generations be born and live and pass in a matter of moments. I have been exposed to historical events to help me understand better what it was I needed to know. I have been allowed to walk beside my body in other lifetimes and watch how I was and who I was, and I have been allowed to see the other side of death. These are cherished and privileged opportunities that somewhere in my life I earned the right to have them. To speak of them to other people is, in a way, disenchanting because it is difficult to convey to people who have never been to those places what it is. I try my best as a storyteller to tell them and still fall short of it.

I also know that the reason that he works with his students the way that he does is because Ramtha never wants to overshadow any of you. In other words, his whole point of focus is to come here and to teach you to be extraordinary. He already is. And it is not about him producing phenomena. If he told you he was going to send you runners, you are going to get them big time. It is not about him doing tricks in front of you. That is not what he is. Those are tools of an avatar that is still a guru that needs to be worshiped, and that is not the case with him.

So what will happen is he will teach you and cultivate you and allow you to create the phenomenon, and you will be able to do that. Then one day when you are able to manifest on cue and you are able to leave your body and you are able to love, when it is to the human interest impossible to do that, he will walk right out here in your life because you are ready to share what he is. And what he is is simply what you are going to become. Until then he is diligent, patient, all-knowing, and all-understanding of everything that we need to know in order to learn to be that.

The one thing I can say to you is that if you are interested in his presentation, and you are starting to love him even though you can't see him, that is a good sign because it means that what was important in you was your soul urging you to unfold in this lifetime. And it may be against your neuronet. Your personality can argue with you and debate with you, but that sort of logic is really transparent when the soul urges you onto an experience.

If this is what you want to do, you are going to have to exercise patience and focus and you are going to have to do the work. The work in the beginning is very hard, but if you have the tenacity to stay with it, then one day I can tell you that this teacher is going to turn you inside out. One day you will be able to do all the remarkable things that you have heard the masters in myth and legend have the capacity to do. You will be able to do them because that is the journey. And ultimately that ability is singularly the reality of a God awakening in human form.

Now that is my journey and it has been my journey all of my life. If it wasn't important and if it wasn't what it was, I certainly wouldn't be living in oblivion most of the year for the sake of having a few people come to have a New Age experience. This is far greater than a New Age experience. I should also say that it is far more important than the ability to meditate or the ability to do yoga. It is about changing consciousness all through our lives on every point and to be able to unhinge and unlimit our minds so that we can be all we can be.

You should also know what I have learned is that we can only demonstrate what we are capable of demonstrating. If you would say, well, what is blocking me from doing that, the only block that we have is our inability to surrender, to allow, and to support ourself even in the face of our own neuronet of doubt. If you can support yourself through doubt, then you will make the breakthrough because that is the only block that stands in your way. And one day you are going to do all these things and get to see all the things that I have seen and been allowed to see.

So I just wanted to come out here and show you that I exist, that I love what I do, and that I hope that you are learning from this teacher. And, more importantly, I hope you continue with it.

— *JZ Knight*

THE SECRETS OF LIFE ARE NOT BEYOND US

From the Lord God of my being to the Lord God of your being, I salute that which is termed you and the God that you are. Greetings.

O my beloved God,
God bless my life,
fill it with your movement,
and bring forth my life
in harmony,
that the destiny of my life
is not given
to my body
but to my Holy Spirit.
So be it.

I want you to know that I am honored to be with you, and what I honor, some of you have not yet even begun to understand. I honor the God that innocently but deliberately wears the body and the personality, and I am honored to be in the midst of such beings.

I am pleased that you celebrated the high holidays in a spirit of joy and thanksgiving and that you took moments out to look upon the tree and see Christ-in-mass, see Point Zero as it pyramids all the way down through all the levels, and the gifts that sit under the tree representing so blatantly the gifts of the Spirit. It is we who put them there, for God is a giver. A high holiday is not simply that which is termed a national holiday, an event for capitalistic purposes. For those who can see, they understand, and it is through their eyes that they find a true reverence and the true meaning of what is around them.

In my life my great teachers were all of the men I conquered, all the people that I loved, all the women that I knew, and every part of every tree that I passed in my journey. They all taught me to pause later in my life and to understand that God is embellished in a leaf and that the secrets of life are not so deep that ordinary men and women cannot perceive them. They are there in the growth of a sapling under a great tree struggling for the light. They are there in the fishes making their way back to their nests to ensure that their children can survive, that they too one day can participate in the Spirit of God in mass. They are there in watching a humble beetle make his journey walking the treacherous road of predators and finding enough foodstuffs to take back to his hovel so that he can be sustained, or watching that which is termed the wildfowl as they land on emerald rivers with crackling reeds and watching them as they choose their mates, very particular, and how they give their life to make their nests and to spend long moments on nurturing the egg, the holy egg, to bring about the young and to care for them unselfishly. Is that not God? That is a great teaching.

When we become aware that we are God, we see life differently. For most of you, you struggle in the raging river of humanity. You are still caught up with the snags of your past. You are caught up with the wounds of your bodies, your neuronets. You are trying to make a crossing but you are afraid of being hurt or that you are going to miss something else that you hold back. So you are caught up on the snags of crossing this river.

Let us look at that then. When we don't know that we are God, there is one thing we do know, that we are human beings. That knowingness is so common that we have yet to have the startling realization that when we know that is what we are, then is it any wonder that we are part of the snags of life that tear at the flesh, that hook upon it, that we are a part of a life that is so encumbered by the flesh that we are afraid to cross the river?

The enlightening aspect of this is, of course, that we have empowered what we think we are. I observed you 35,000 years ago. I have observed you recently because, as it is seen, every moment is up for change. There is nothing set except the divine that can set it for the ignorant, and they can only set it for the ignorant according to the ignorant. The divine has never been able to set the divine for the divine.

I have watched you and observed you because when you don't know you are being observed is when you are the most real. Then I know what student I have and I know what potential you are collapsing and what you are really wanting to live. I know what is your common nature. That is the most powerful choice because that means God must flow through the common nature of the human being. I watch you pass great teachings every day. And you know why you pass them? Because you never see them. You know what you see? You see your bodies, your faces. You see how fit or fat your bodies are. You think about eating, sleeping, and copulating. You think about clothes. You think about all of this. Now that says to me, in simple human terms, that you made a choice to see only what benefits your flesh. That says to me, as it were, that you have ignored your God. You make a choice every day that you wake up to either see the body and its personality or see the God.

Now there are a handful of you — and we can put them on one hand and have fingers left over — who every day are learning commonly to see God. That means that every day is a lesson to them. Lessons do not have to be hard. Lessons can be marvelously astounding. To be astounded is a pleasurable experience. To be caught up in something so simple but able to see its mechanism is an astounding experience. There are a few of you that have taken on the common nature of seeing what you are, what you want to be, God. Well, how do we see God in its highest, purest, most unconvoluted way? In nature, and when you get up and you walk and you look around, you rejoice in the morning light. Some of you don't rejoice in the morning light because it is raining outside, but that is your human. I want you to know that. Your human doesn't rejoice in anything uncomfortable but your God rejoices in it because it is the waters of life. It nourishes the earth. And when do you say it is too much? It will never be enough.

The second they get up they inhale the breath of life and rejoice in their liveliness. If what we are mirrors exactly what is in our life, then what are you? A person who in common thought doesn't have to be reminded, doesn't have to go to a note card that says "Look upon nature today; therein you shall see God." A person who doesn't have to do that, who wakes up and sees that, is now an entity who has elected by simple choice to see themselves connected to everything rather than isolated in a human form.

Yet here is the paradox. Such an entity who finds the lessons in nature becomes a lover of nature. We only observe what we truly love or hate. So if we have an entity who is observing nature, then that entity is observing itself — how beautiful — because what they are then is the union of the whole. Now that is a master in the making, quietly doing it. That entity then is going to have a different reality than the human entity because that entity can make the crossing across the river and will walk on the water because they are the water. The human being will go to the water and say, "I command you to be still and I will make a bridge to cross you." The peculiar thing about human beings is that everything is done for self-glory. But who is the self they glorify? It is the human, the personality: "I can build it bigger and better."

That is like my army around the great tree, the Lord of the Forest.[1] I begged them, "What does this tree know that you don't know?" They couldn't answer that question because these are warriors. How could they be intimidated

---

1 See "Ramtha's Autobiography, I Had no Teacher but Nature" in *A Beginner's Guide to Creating Reality,* 3rd ed. (Yelm: JZK Publishing, a division of JZK, Inc., 2004).

by such an obviously mammoth being? How could that thing know more than they? So because their altered ego got in the way, they couldn't find the answer and yet it was staring at them. They couldn't even see it. That is what you are. That is how you are.

"And this tree does not know how to die; only you know how to do that. This tree shall be alive when your generations to generations to generations, yet unborn, will be here."

"Ah, but, Lord, we can cut this tree down in a moment."

"Not a moment. It will take you longer than a moment to cut the heart out of this tree. And that is true, you can do that, but that is the difference between you and the tree. You know how to die; it doesn't."

The Difference between Hearing the Words and Applying Them

In observing you, because you came here to learn the spiritual life, to learn the power of consciousness and energy and how to correct some problems in your life, I want you to know in a very candid and uninvolved way that you don't listen to me. You filter out only what the human needs and you don't hear everything else. What is the difference then in hearing the words and the application? If you had heard everything I have taught you and if you had applied yourself forthrightly and applied everything I have taught you with due diligence and discharged that reality properly, then whatsoever you have created you will have a crossing and all your dreams will come true. But you don't listen to me.

To understand why some of your dreams are not going to come true, there are some of you who insist on doing it your own way. I beg to ask you, you do not know better than I do, because if you did you wouldn't be sitting where you are and I where I am. But there is a willfulness to the human psyche that is interesting. Everyone strives for uniqueness. That is the reason why we have a word called beauty and a word called ugly. Now in the true kingdom of God those words would never even be there. They would be unnecessary because they are not aspects of God. They are aspects of the human.

There is a need for individuality, yet the complexity is that you want to be individual enough but you want to blend. You want to be an individual but you want to be accepted. Accepted by whom, other individuals? So with this need to be an individual and to stand on your own two feet, what comes with that is a fool. And the fool says, "I know what is best for myself and I can cull out all of this garbage because it is not where I want to be in my life. I want to be an individual. I do not want to be homogenized in the Spirit. I worked too hard to be individualistic."

So here is what happens. You only take what you want to take and what you think is good for you. I have never taught you one teaching that did not benefit you or one teaching that did not evolve you if utterly embraced. I am not here to take you backwards. I am here to take you forward into the beautiful, marvelous, and lovely present, which you keep missing.

In this need for individuality you set up your own rules and I must teach you around those rules. Then when we come to create a new year, how would you set it up? What tools, I beg to ask, have you cultivated last year that will allow you to fulfill with absolute certitude what it is you want? And I will say to you tonight you are crippled.

Why is it that your life as an individual is so messed up and your life as the spiritual only helps you, it seems, at the strangest of times and on things that don't even seem to matter? Why isn't the Spirit full-bore with you? Because you set up the terms. You set up the neuronet. You have barred the wall from full expression, full participation.

The Void washes us, don't you know? When we enter the Void, we cannot enter in flesh and blood. This pretty little face can't go there, that beautiful body can't go there, and yet these are the terms that we set up for self. And to be able to focus is too damn uncomfortable for this beautiful little face and that beautiful little body. So you know what you do? You don't even try. You get to a place and you just sit there and think. Why didn't you get there? Because you don't listen and because you don't do the work. You expect me to do the work for you. That is not what this school is about. I already did the work. I lived the life. I walked the walk. This is yours to do. So how hard is it? It is not hard at all. It is as simple as the choices that you have made in your life.

THE TEACHINGS THREATEN OUR PERSONALITY

You really need some help because you don't have faith in the work. You ruined it because you took it only to the degree that it would not embarrass, demean, or shrivel your individual identity. And when you did that, the identity was more important than the Holy Spirit. When you need the teachings, you don't have faith in them because you don't do them. So ultimately what we must look at is why ask for something you are not worthy of. You are not worthy of the Holy Spirit, nor are you worthy for resolve, nor are you worthy to walk on the water, that raging river that is going to make a crossing between our humanity and our Spirit.

There is no other place — and I beg you to go and find one if you think I am in error — that could have delivered to you finer teachings and finer disciplines and with utter grace, strength, and tenacity than what you have been given. But you seem to think that the teachings threaten you physically. They do. They threaten the personality. When the personality needs to have its seed spilt, its orgasms, its belly full, its hair slicked back, and its fine clothes on, the teachings get in the way. All of these are sensual feedbacks, and the more sensual feedbacks we have, the more beautiful we are or the more acceptable we are. That is just the way it works.

You seem to think the teachings threaten you. Well, they do because they are asking you to replace this altered ego with the kingdom of heaven. Yeshua ben Joseph said, when he was adored for the miracles that he did, "It isn't I who did this." What he was saying is, "It wasn't me, Yeshua ben Joseph, who did this. Don't worship my altered ego. Don't worship my face. Don't worship my feet. Don't worship my garment. Don't you understand? It was the heavenly Father within me that did this. I am nothing." He never took credit for the work. He always gave it to his God and by doing so reached some test you will never do in this lifetime, because you cannot stand up and say it is my God who has done this because it is too hard to deny the credit to your personality. It is too tempting. I guess that is the difference and the reason why masters do not come and dwell amongst you. We only get in our life what we are. We only manifest in our life what we are equal to. That is the law. It is across the board. It is without prejudice. You get everything that you want and, unfortunately, you are wanting things that are perishable. I am endeavoring to teach you of the imperishable.

Many amongst you have done miracles, but is that enough to sit on for the rest of your days? "Well, I was able to do this. Two years ago I did this, I did that." Are you going to ride on that reputation? Does that somehow excuse your behavior today and why you can't get rid of your headache today? Is the fact that you were a miracle-worker last year going to cause you to somehow skate by your problem you created today? Reputation is not going to resolve life. It is being it every moment in the divine present.

I cannot teach anyone who insists on hearing only what they want to hear. I can teach those who wake up and understand that their real problem in life is that they have been given enormous wisdom, and not only did they hear it verbally but they were discharged to enact it. And to your credit most were able to do it and prove to themselves that the teaching is not a philosophy but is a truth.

I could sit down and weep for 35,000 more years that the grandest crossing I made was to come back to get you to do that one miraculous little thing that is truth, and if that doesn't do it, nothing is going to do it. It isn't then so much am I Ramtha or am I not but that I taught you how to do the miraculous, and you did it. Does that not beg the question how much more is there? That one little miracle, those two little miracles, those two levels of truth are like feathers in the wind when it comes to the personality, because the personality can deny, reject, and reason the miraculous into its own sordid terms of logic. It happened to the best of you. Remember that saying, "The first will become last and the last will become first"? It is so utterly true.

Somewhere there must be born in each of you, as was born in me, that there has got to be something better than my life. I had a lot of time to think about that for seven years on the rock. I sat and suffered for seven years. And I want to tell you something that you should make noteworthy: I created my own betrayal because in one instance I didn't use my wisdom. How many times a day do you not use your wisdom? Do I need to point out to you the abuse you heap upon your life by not using the wisdom that you somewhere have inside of you that you gained one startling day?

The first few years I was filled with anger and bitterness. I resented and hated. I resented everybody and hated everyone. I was the ultimate victim. Because I was the leader, I made a great fall from my immortality, the legend that I was. Imagine that. You see, I know why you don't do things that threaten your persona, because I did too. I know what it feels like. I resented, I hated, and yet I could do nothing about it. So sit there and resent and hate a little more, Ram. You only create the next day that is going to hurt you even more and you are going to feel worse. And after a while I got tired of feeling worse. You know what I resented? I resented falling from my image, not to mention the wound. I resented that. But there was nothing I could do about it because, after all, I created the circumstances of my own fall. Just like you keep creating the circumstances that keep coming around in your life, so did I.

That night bird taught me more than I had ever learned in my entire life. It was my one and true companion. It didn't really care that I was the Ram, just don't make any noise and wake up the children. After a while I obeyed that. I was in their territory; they weren't in mine. Interesting.

Do you know what resentment is about? It is trying to revisit the past. There is a savage quality in the personality about wanting to go back to its past. It is savage enough to where you keep going back to the things that are familiar to you, thought-forms that are familiar, ways of thinking that are familiar. It is a savage element in you. I know. It was in me.

Now let me tell you what that is like. You keep reaffirming your past because you elected to do it. That is why it gets in the way of the miraculous in your life, because the miraculous must in its brilliance pass through the shadows of your personality. Going back to the past would be like me going back to the last city that I had just razed to the ground, rebuilding it and destroying it again, then thinking about it and going back and redoing it. The past, to me, like you do every day would be trying to go back to Onai, raise it up, bring it back from where it had floated off to, spend all of my time rebuilding, stone by stone — not to mention, of course, raising people from the dead — building it back up so I could have it suppress me again.

Why would I want to raise up the warrior who spat in my eye? Why would I want to raise up the satrap who shamed my brother? Why would I want to do that? Well, you say, you wouldn't. But I tell you, isn't that what you do? Don't you keep rebuilding your past? You do. You say the faces have changed, but I tell you it would be no different than if I could move to another plane, grab those people that I murdered out of the current life they are in, they disappear and they move back into the past. All you are doing is recycling the same old faces. That is all you are doing. They are just wearing a different mask.

It still hasn't really occurred to you, my beloved people — except for those few that I can count on one hand and have fingers left over — that to me reality begins in the mind. It is not in the physical. That is not reality. That is the difference between the people that are hung-up on the snags on a raging river. Their reality is the raging river.

This River Passing Is Treacherous

The beings that have lived their life in communion with all life, their reality is not one specific thing but the communion of life itself. If I said to you it is not what you are doing, it is what you are thinking, then that would be succinctly following the teachings that consciousness and energy creates reality. If you have thought it, you have already done it.

Now how do we take that statement and put it in context to the miraculous? What you think in your brain is always manifesting. I call it common thought. Common thought is the most powerful thought of all because it has no objection. It is allowed to be. The miraculous we must labor on, move energy up past our first three seals, sit there, and do it. It is treacherous because we may get tired, it may be late, we could be in bed, or we could be laying some harlot. So it is always treacherous. This river passing is treacherous. But, you see, this is what happens. Your past was like my past. I stood on the shoulders of my conquests, but when they were removed I had no shoulders to stand on. That was my common thought.

Your common thought is your altered ego. That is why it keeps manifesting, and that is why we have to work so hard to get the Holy Spirit to move in our life. We say this is hard work. Yes, it is, because these words are still not yours. These thoughts that are delivered eloquently and forthrightly are still not your thoughts. You don't think like I do. Even in this brain of this woman I think as a God. I am using the brain as a God. How else do you explain those hours of orientation that flow? That is the mind of God flowing through a human brain that you could pick apart easily but you can't argue that it is flowing. I am demonstrating to you common thought. It is ushering from me in unlimited measure. You can't even hold a conversation with me. Your past is reinforced by the commonness of your personality, and the miraculous is still not your thoughts. You don't think as God; therefore you can't live as God.

It is not what you do; it is what you think. And I as your teacher tell you that your thoughts to me are reality. I don't care what you do afterwards. It is insignificant. The point of reality was created in your brain, and you entertained the thought. You are a fool if you think that those thoughts are not open to everyone on the light plane and beyond. You are a fool if you think that they are private. They are not private.

So the pretense of divinity is only going to take you to the grave, and here you have lost a body that enables you to do the wonderful works of the kingdom of heaven. I come back to the statement: Why are you so afraid of your personality? Why do you think you are going to lose life by being a divine being? What a silly and foolish remark.

And there is no excuse to say, "Well, I am young." That is not an excuse. Youth offers the greatest store of energy of all for the performance of Christ-in-mass. When you are older it is hard to get your bones to quit aching because so much of your emotional life is now in them. It is even more difficult when you are not virile to find the energy that is lost hormonally in the body, to resurrect it in a sort of passion that you knew only when you were young and reckless. Everyone thinks they are indestructible when they are young. It is those hormones that make you think that, but they are being abused and not used.

What are the rewards? The kingdom of heaven. What could that possibly be? It means that the mind is laid on the altar of God and it is laid there for God to purely take up and work through as an instrument of creating paradise. When we come to that point we must lay a heavy burden on that altar, which is hard to do because it is hard to lay down our illnesses because they have been our personality. It is hard to lay down our sexuality because it has caused us to have problems in our life that have given meaning to our life. Problems always are a reason to live.

It is hard to lay down the sexuality. It is hard to lay down the feminine identity because it has gotten you so far in life. But I tell you, one day it will get you nowhere. It is very hard to lay down the masculine identity because then you think you are missing youth. I beg you to reason with me what one thing you have not done that you keep doing. Let's take your habits. When do you get enough? You get enough when you do it once, but if that is not enough I would beg you to reason with me — bare your logic to me and I will listen to you — how the repetitiveness of that life activity could possibly be greater than the life of a master. It is not.

Does it mean that you are afraid you won't be loved? If you are holding onto love via your body, your looks, your youth, or whatever has worked for you that causes you to have those people in your life, if you are afraid that you are going to lose that for the kingdom of heaven, then you don't deserve the kingdom of heaven and you have got the wrong people in your life. If we take it back further I would say your thoughts have created them all, so your thoughts are in error because no matter what you think in your brain must be played out here in the faces of everyone that is in your life.

It is a lot to lay on the altar. It is a lot to trust God. But God isn't about trusting; God is about being. Trust is only when you are separate from something. You can never mistrust what you are, which is only when you are separated from you, and you are separated. No one can ever mistrust themselves because they always live what it is their self is, whether it is the human or the God. You can never mistrust what you are. You can predict what you will be by your thoughts. But when it comes to another, that is a sign of separateness. That is a discharge of trust. In God there is no trusting; there is only being.

Now this is the way it is. I don't know in my long career how to tell you more simply you have chosen your thoughts and you choose to have them every day as common thought. Understand this: There should be no surprises in your life because nothing comes to your life that you didn't first think, contemplate, and fantasize as common thought, the most powerful thought of all. Don't you look at me and say, "I was innocent of this." No, you weren't. You stand up and be counted. You are a creator, and take credit for it because you had the fantasy, you pondered the thought, you wondered, you plotted, you manipulated, you were clever, and now you have got it in all of those complexities. How much simpler can I say that?

I would be utterly out of place if I told you these were the loftiest teachings there ever were without you demonstrating them for yourself. Since you have been the miraculous in those splendid moments, that is why I am here to tell you they work, and they work all the way across the board.

You lay a lot on the altar of God, but when you cross the river you will see it was nothing. You are all going to cross the river because you are all going to die. When you cross and you are caught up out of this body — and out of its neuronet stuck with its habits — and you take a look backwards, you are going to understand what I am telling you. Perhaps it will have to take another one of these lifetimes to get you to see.

There are some who think that I am on your case. Yes, I am, and why shouldn't I be? I am your teacher. I am telling you what no one else can tell you, not even your best friend because they never tell you anything. They always tell you things that benefit themselves.

You are going to have to replace your mind from the popular world of altered ego, its comings and goings, its images, its expectations. You are going to have to replace some of that world with being God, creating a world and making changes in it. Then you get to walk through the marketplace and know that you affected it instead of going through it just to have a good time. The greatest time, as it were, is no-time. To walk through a marketplace and have no-time means that you have changed it. That is the greatest gift of all. The marketplace is never going to give you a better time than the one you are going to create, I assure you.

If you say you are a serious God of the Great Work, you must dedicate some of your life to being that God. And that doesn't mean that you have to walk around in a long robe and espouse empty words. It means that you have to live the substance of it and be righteous, the right use of.

WHAT DOES IT MEAN TO BE PURE IN SPIRIT?

There is a saying that is so utterly true. It says the pure in Spirit see God. Let's think about that statement, the pure in Spirit. What does that mean? How come you couldn't feel the presence of the Holy Spirit? Because you are not pure in Spirit. That means that you set up games and trapdoors in your mind and conditions on how you will be spiritual. That is what that means. A person who is clever, manipulating, and takes only from this what they wish and nothing else is not pure in Spirit.

We could take a common person out on the street who has never heard the teachings, a common entity who has always been straightforward and has never manipulated people, and say it is an honest man or an honest woman. Some people have the need to say that honesty is brutal. Honesty isn't brutal. It is sweet. It is rare. All of you think that saying no is being honest. Did you know that saying yes is also honest? Is that not flavorful? There are some of you who think that being mean comes with being honest. It isn't. It is compassion. It is beauty, true beauty. When a person is honorable to you, they are pure in Spirit. They don't have to be in this school. Pure in Spirit means there are no shadows which the answer is passing through, no labyrinth through which it will come out deformed and muddy.

When a person is honorable with you, you don't have to play their game and get caught up in their life to try to find the solution. An honorable woman is pure in Spirit and they have cleansed themselves, whether by their upbringing or the circumstances that they are in. They have never been haunted by their past. When we are haunted by our past is when we have been dishonest with ourself and never looked at the truth in ourself. The reason we have nightmares is that we have never been honest with ourself and said what we really are. We have always played cloak-and-dagger and hide-and-seek with ourself, and why? To be charming, I am certain, to be liked, to be mysterious, to be clever. All of that game-playing, all of that manipulation, has destroyed the purity of Spirit.

The entity who lives in the backwater and can be honorable tells no lies, and you tell a great deal of them. You create rumors, you lie, and you are dishonest because you don't know what it is to be honorable. You don't know what it is to simply speak your truth. Yet the practice therein of doing that brings about righteousness in the individual.

Why do I bring that up? Because deception is the game of the altered ego. Deception is the game. As long as we can keep them out here occupied under the delusion that we are what we say we are, then they will never pass a certain line to find out what we don't even know that we are.

What does that have to do with consciousness and energy creating reality? Unrighteousness causes a splintering of focused energy because every time you focus, it must focus through the labyrinth of dishonesty and unrighteousness. It is that pure energy that is always squeezed through the dirty rag and so the pure water that was once brought in comes out muddy and dirty at the other end. And you say, "What happened? It didn't work." The teachings are not going to work for you until you are pure in Spirit — that is being honest and honorable — that when you go to bed at night you are not troubled by your dreams and you are never troubled about what did you say to this person and remember what you said to that person and try to keep the trap going.

The more honorable and honest that you are, the cleaner you are. Then when we add common thought of the mind of God, we have instantaneous manifestation. Your manifestations that you have spent long hours focusing on have manifested in a splintered fashion. If you become enlightened on this, you will see that it lit up every part of the labyrinth of your mind instead of going straight to the center. You will understand that you cannot possibly manifest anything in your life without it having to go through the labyrinth of the mind.

Do you really expect that focusing on the miraculous should appear immediately? If consciousness and energy are the ultimate ground of all reality, then what have we done with our consciousness and what are the rules of manifestation here? The rules are not anything that we wrote but the way we think and, alas, we find the fly in the inkwell. We understand that only until we are pure in Spirit can we get pure instant manifestation. And why was it that the little insignificant things happened in our life and it seemed like none of the big things did? Because the big things take a lot of plotting and planning and the little things are so insignificant they don't need a labyrinth because they are not important. That is why they happen.

Why is it one day you can heal your headache and the next day you can't? Because the headache has contingencies on it. We have to first get past why we elected to have the headache and how having the headache benefited us. Perhaps we didn't want to work that day. Perhaps the headache is the result of stress. Where did the stress come from? The stress came from mistrust. Where did the mistrust come from? Separateness, no unity in God. How then can we heal the headache until we have healed the problem behind it, until we have cleaned out the labyrinth that goes to it? So the ancient word is the pure in heart and the pure in Spirit always see God.

So what should you be doing? If I were you — and I am happy I am not — instead of working for fabulous wealth I would work on all the detours that keep me from my God and keep me from being it. And what would that be? My own dishonesty, the games I play with myself. What are some of the examples? When are you going to stop blaming your parents for your miserable life, and why do you keep carrying that around as a crutch? Because it gets you where you want. That is what clever people do. They can use it to get what they want. Do you understand how the game works now? Righteous people don't do that; clever people do. It is part of the game plan. It is part of an attack. Every time you do that, it would be equal to me going back and building up the city of Onai just to destroy it again. How ridiculous that is. You do the same thing but at the cost of the kingdom of heaven, at the cost of, in the final analysis, torment.

If I were you I would work on the righteousness and purity of Spirit. Every day you squeeze five minutes out of your day — I know it is going to be hard — to be totally present and say, "Holy Spirit, my Holy Spirit, of this day I do beseech you to present to me the quagmire of my dishonesty and feed it to me until I have consumed it all and there is none left." Hard to do, but if you are going to go into immortality, you don't have any other choice because that is what is keeping you from that.

The second thing I would do is learn to be righteous, the right use of focus. What does that mean? That means stop thinking in terms of your altered ego and think in terms of the light of all eternity.[2] This life that you are living, there are some of you that don't know how close you are going to come to dying. Very close. This life could be over tomorrow morning and you haven't even lived it. You think living life is bedding down with every whore. You think life is visiting every Prancing Pony Inn. You think life is drugs. That is not life. Then you have missed life again.

I would start thinking in terms of the light of all eternity. What this moment is worth in the light of all eternity would be my next focus. What is it I am about to say? Is what I am about to say befitting for the present moment and the trouble I am in, or is what I am about to say befitting for

2 See also "In the Light of All Eternity, What Is This Moment Worth?" in
A Master's Key for Manipulating Time, Fireside Series, Vol. 2, No. 2
ed. (Yelm: JZK Publishing, a division of JZK, Inc., 2002).

the light of all eternity? I would always choose the light of all eternity because, remember, ultimately our prosecutors are ourselves, the hangman is ourself. Why should we beg deliverance from them, which is ourself, for a temporal life when we can have life for all eternity? In the light of all eternity, what is this moment worth?

The next thing I would do is not be taking from people and playing the game of mental prostitution. There are some of you here that are so stingy. You are greedy thieves. Well, what is to be said of that? How can you ask for fabulous wealth when you are greedy with the wealth that you have? How can you be God and covet your purse?

There are those of you here who are thieves. You steal from people and call it manifestation. See how the labyrinth works? See how we justify everything and that the personality must be justified in order to be enabled to hold onto this life? I tell you not all the money in this world and the world to come is worth losing your purity of Spirit. It just isn't. There are many a saint that walked and ate unleavened bread, drank only water and sometimes didn't even have that, and wine would have been a delight beyond measure. Who did this and why did they do this? Because it was the principle of their life. They could have the wine, the oily feast, the mutton, the sweetmeat, the olives and cheese but only if they knew how to travel in certain circles and to do that called for a clouding of purity of Spirit. Great beings sometimes elect to be simple because to be otherwise means to give up what is nearer and dearer to them, the light of all eternity.

To the extreme of that, there are those of you who are thieves. I have watched you. Didn't you feel your conscience move? Yes, you did. You know what you did with it? You justified it as a manifestation. It isn't yours unless it is given to you and given to you through God's love — God is a giver and not a taker — and it is given to you without expectation in return. That is unconditional and unlimited. You are going to find very few people in the world that know how to give like that, so the taking may be very far and few between. Everything should be weighed against your spiritual life.

Don't you take a golden cup or a copper penny that isn't yours and if you have, you give it back. That is called honesty and being honorable. It is hard to do, hard to swallow one's shame. I would rather swallow my shame and know that I was going to live forever — perhaps mock my own ridicule and my own peers — I would rather live up to that than go to the worm, have my memory gone, be born again with no recollection, and have to start this all over again with a wounded soul.

When the Miraculous Becomes Common

God, make me a giver.
Let that which flows
through me
flow through me unlimited.

That is what you need to work on. If you are a diligent student you will find that sometimes being honest is finally admitting that you love them. Honesty doesn't have to be brutal or hard. It is a moment where the soul leaps in jubilation because it is free of the shadows.

If you do all of this you will make room for common thought. If you strive every day for the loftiest thought of all, you do not have to walk around like a mummy but you are going to have to walk around aware. You are going to have to lay aside your despair, your victimization, your altered ego, and to live like God intended us all to live. You are going to have to find compassion, love, mercy, and charity every day. When you do, then you can say, "This day I was truly alive," and so it will be.

When we have cleaned the soul, we have cleaned the mind. All karma is, is an unclean mind recorded for the next lifetime. Then when I talk to you, you can listen to me plainly, simply, and clearly because there is nothing clouding your thoughts. There is no diversion there. There is no threat to your altered ego. It will be pure in Spirit. You shall be utterly amazed at how much you will hear and how much you will embrace. And the more you embrace, the greater life is. Then you will have found you have begun living as common thought, that the common thought is the lofty thought instead of as it is now, that the common thought is the limited thought and the lofty thought is the miraculous. When the miraculous is common, you know you have made progress.

Impact of the Master Teacher's Words on the Brain

I cannot make you be masters, and most of you never will be. You will only take and apply teachings that are good and beneficial to your life, and that is all right. We have moved you, as it were, off of a line potential. Every time I talk to you and you listen to me, this is how it works: I verbalize the words, and that nerve that moves from your inner ear into your brain is carrying a vibration. The audio nerve then sets up thought-forms in the brain. In order for you to hear me, you must be forming thoughts of what I am saying. If you haven't formed thoughts of what I have said, you haven't heard me. This is why the teacher is so important because the teacher will tell you what you don't know or what you know but have never organized.

What is the beauty of that? When you are hypnotically with me this moment and I talk to you and you listen to me, it means that you are creating the thought-forms that have no obstruction. Why is that important? Because when you think according to the way I talk, you have changed your linear life potential. We have moved you two degrees. How many potentials lie from this present to a two-degree potential? How many incidents are avoided? How many problems are left behind? How many opportunities are sitting on the next life potential? You have all of these potentials simultaneously. It can be changed at any moment. But what is the mechanism of change? How you think. Why is listening so important? Because in order to hear me you have to think about the words I am saying, and while you are doing that you are reorganizing your linear life potential and we have just moved you off from the life you had.

Where am I moving you to? I certainly wouldn't be moving you to something less than what you already are.

You don't get any lower than what you are. We only move to something greater. Your science has proven it with a handful of my students, including my daughter. It is scientific fact now. So if you listened to me and formed all the words as thought-forms in your brain, that means you were consciously creating reality and I was your teacher leading you to think that way. Who benefits? You do. So be it.

How many of you can envision your life without the learning that you have gained in the Great Work? What would your life be like had you not heard these teachings this lifetime and therefore did not respond to them? It is a curious but compelling question, indeed, after talking about the topic of the pure at heart — the pure in Spirit, the righteous — and referring to the shadows, those aspects of the human personality/altered ego that prevent the crossing. If you were honorable in answering this question with full-thrust honesty instead of answering only what you feel you could tolerate, then by answering this question correctly you have more than likely found one of your shadows, because one of the shadows that you hold onto is regret. And with that, there is a twist of the regret that resents the need to make a crossing. So the way that we then begin to see our own insecurities and inadequacies is to reflect upon what-if.

Many of you answered along these lines: I was very successful. I was doing very well as a capitalist or a socialist. I had a lot of money in the bank. I lived in a beautiful home. I was married or was free, whichever. I had a very successful life. I had a very successful social circle. I was an entity of aspiring prominence among my peers. I had a beautiful wife or husband, beautiful children. I was free. I owned nothing. I lived off of what I could. I did whatever I wanted to. I came and went as I pleased. I was famous, adored, imitated, rich. I was poor, indigent.

In crossing the river you have to lay the altered ego on the altar in order to be free enough to walk on the water to pass it. Sometimes entities don't really realize why their great manifestations don't work. It is because they are manifesting always and every moment is a manifestation of the moment before. When it comes to the big important issues and why they seem to procrastinate or be postponed, we begin to wonder what is it in us that prevents this from occurring, and I can tell you straightaway it is that you are not honest people, you are not pure in Spirit. What that means is that there are neuronets of the shadow aspect. The shadow aspect is what we endeavor to hide behind the mask, and those are due in part to resentment.

You resent losing your prominence. You can talk all you want to about what a relief it was, but if you were honest you would find that one of the issues that plagues you is your need for it, and in this you had a fall from it. When you had all of the money that you wanted and the fine hovel and the automachines and all of that, there was a prestige in it that seemingly now you have lost. But prestige is a lacquering of the altered ego. It is what polishes it. When you take that away, there is a resentment that lingers inside the entity.

If you answered the question honestly you would say, "Well, I lost the love of my life, I lost my children, I abandoned them, I lost my freedom, I cannot come and go." There is a resentment in it and this unconscious resentment never shows itself until one becomes the barest of honesty to oneself. It is important to find these aspects that are the shadows of the altered ego because when the light of the Spirit is shining forward, the flow of consciousness is ready to collapse energy into the perfect form of reality. What happens is it is moving with such rapidity, such beauty, and such intent, because it knows no other way — there is no such thing as unintentional consciousness — that it comes up against the bulwark of what is called resentment and the resentment stops its emergence and stands in its way. We call it lack.

The need to come to an event and then go out there and act like a heathen is sustaining what I am telling you.

When I say heathen, you go out there and forget that you are to live as a lofty thought and you return to the social scene in full ritual garb. You have just gone back, because that is really the place that you get polished. You don't get polished in the spiritual in the world. It is that very element of the personality that prevents the emergence of bread in hand, because there are other things that are coagulated and standing in its way. I tell you, as illusionary as this sounds, it is very real because these are the tics and tacks that make up the personality.

You have to address resentment, and this is tied to your past. This is where the past starts to take on a colorful façade and dimension. When you ask yourself that question, and if you are honest, then the past starts to come out into the light. Now we see what we have always considered forbidden about ourself that caused us to be such game-players, so clever, so mysterious. We were endeavoring to cover up something that we were afraid to look at. We are afraid to be honest even with ourself but I tell you, unless you have that, you will never have clarity. You will never be pure. There are no secrets in the kingdom of heaven, there just aren't, and you cannot hold them and still be the master you are hoping to be on the other side of resentment. You are having a terrible time becoming it because it does demand the laying on the altar such heinous aspects of self. It requires, as painful, as ugly, and as smelly as it is, that you pull them out and look at them.

No one is perfect. I was never a saint in my life, but I am the first one to tell you I wasn't. The less I pretended, which I never did do, the more honest I was. That allowed a razor focus in me because there is nothing that stood in the way of my desire. There is nothing that inhibited it. There is nothing that curbed my appetite. There is nothing that diminished my fearlessness — nothing.

There is a lot to you that you hide and that you are afraid to know and, more terrifying, that you are afraid somebody else will know. Don't you know that everyone I know in the greater echelons of consciousness can see everything you are? It is like the blind man walking around in a dirt cloud because he is filthy and he is the only one that can't see it. He suspects it because something always smells peculiar about himself but he can't see it.

So if you had never heeded that word and that calling, what would your life have been like? It is beautiful and allowable and preferable to take it and run the linear line with it because then you start to catch those places that are harbored in you that are called unfinished business. The only reason they are unfinished is because they were squelched behind a dirty little door. That is all.

BREAK ON THROUGH TO THE OTHER SIDE

No one can ever make the crossing with an ulterior motive. You will never make it. No one is going to be a full-blown master until they leave no footprints. And you know what footprints are, my beloved people? They are the brambles of the path that lead back to your past. They are always within you and you revisit them every day. You walk backwards. You are trying to rebuild the city of Onai that I destroyed. You are trying to rebuild your past every single day. You walk back and forth. You are walking backwards every day. You wake up in the present, but then you leave it and go and rebuild that which is termed the old temples of thought, and you keep them there.

A master leaves no footprints. That means that the master has no past, none. Is that not a mysteriously rich statement? How can any of you not have a past? Simple: Find no reason to visit it and it will disappear, but that takes some work. That takes an utterly awake person to know when they are walking backwards and when they are walking forwards and when they are walking not at all. The first way we do that is we pull up the dirty little roots that line the causeway to the past and your experiences there that keep you going backwards to search for a reason to be alive in the present.

Stop resenting that you have to give up your victimization of your childhood. Stop it. You are going to find that that is a heavy one in your life because it has gotten you where you are today. It has allowed you to feed as a result of it. And every time you do a little blunder that is embarrassing, that you actually slip and your mask falls down and we see the monster behind it, you run all the way back to your past and start pointing and saying, "Well, this is the reason that I am this way." Stop it. How can you have the power to manifest the kingdom of heaven if you are running back to your childhood to blame everything that is present on the past? You are leaving dirty little footprints. When you pull up that childhood experience, your parents can finally rest in peace and, moreover, so will you. You have to cut it out. We do not revisit childhood experiences. We do not revisit pain. We don't do that any longer. Thou shalt not revisit pain. Thou shalt not cut open the scar. Stop it. That is a footprint to the past.

Stop going backwards to make sense of that which is termed your thoughts today. Stop using the past as the metaphor for the present. Why can you not simply have a thought that is based in nothing but the present? Stop going backwards to find reasons for having such a thought. And you are going to find, my beloved people, a clarity and an honesty starting to shine in you. Moreover, what you are so afraid that you are going to uncover, you need to uncover it. And when you take a look at it you will understand that it is part of the past journey. When I tell you don't go back there any longer, you will never have to think in terms of your past again. You will be liberated from it. That is what I want. That is utter clarity in which analogical mind happens in the twinkling of an eye. When you are that pure, you move to a state of analogical mind instantly because there is nothing standing in the way.

Here is what it is like talking to someone earnestly, passionately, and openly. You are about to make a point and they interrupt you and say, "That reminds me of an experience I had ten years ago," and they start babbling on. You might as well not even be there because they have left your presence. That is what it is like.

Being Totally Present in the Moment

When you get rid of the need to excuse yourself, you will stay present and you will turn analogical in the moment. There are no footprints in an analogical moment. Footprints are only measured in the past. A footprint is never measured in the moment. How can you measure someone's footprints when they are standing on them? If you can take that and then apply it, which encourages self-honesty and being vulnerable to self-criticism, that is what it is going to be.

You are going to have to look at yourself and say, "This is what I am, and where am I with this? I got this by the life I have lived." If you don't like that, stop living the life you have lived. Now we begin to understand the word "change." Now we begin to understand you must be born again.

Stop blaming your parents. If you have a resentment that is lingering and you cannot discharge that resentment, then you should go fulfill the resentment. You should do it straightaway and put the pedal to the metal, because that resentment will always stand in the way of your moments of glory. It will rob you of them, and for what? An idea of what could have been. It is very difficult to imagine oneself pastless, but that is exactly what you should do.

Leaving no footprints only abolishes the contention in the family, the blame, the guilt, the remorse, the shame, the arrogance. It only dismisses and washes them away. And what you find is not a mother and father but Gods, people in life who have difficulties living out their own resentments. You never take them on yourself. You never feel blame because they have taken them on themselves. You never feel guilty. You never feel shame. You allow them.

Well, what does that do for your job? You stop living in the past and you just might find you are a genius in the present. If you stop living in the past, you may just find you have energy in the present. Did you know that when you leave no footprints and practice that daily, there is no reference in yourself for inability? There is none. Where would inability come from? Moreover, when you practice this, what can you not do? There is no reference that showed you in the past that you were only capable of the objective of certain things. If you don't have that as a reference point, what can you not do?

I will tell you something else. When you discharge your past and refuse to lay down those footsteps and refuse to go there every day, no longer visiting it, you may find that the unhappiness you suffered all of those years will suddenly be lost in the present and an unequal freedom and joy will start to emerge. Why? Because there are no journeys backwards anymore. You may find that all along you really were a happy soul and needed to express that.

Joy is already in you. It is the radiance of the Spirit of God that moves through you. It is the shadows of resentment, guilt, and anger, the shadows of self-failure and lack that block its splendid light. When we remove them, the light and the presence of the Holy Spirit is full force. That is what we call the pure in mind, the pure in Spirit, the pure in body.

Pure in body has nothing to do with diet. Pure in body means that the body is resilient to the mind, resilient, pliable, and allowing to the Spirit, and it works like a harp. When the quiver of the hand of the Spirit moves across the brain, the mind, the body of the self, strums a harmonic chord, and that is joy. Imagine, it is not something you have to work to be. You are already that. You have been layered by backward thinking. When there is none, there is room to be the Holy Spirit.

Here is something else you should know. You will never heal yourself if you live in resentment of what could have been in your past. You will never, ever heal yourself. Moreover, the greatest group in this audience could only alleviate your misery for moments, but it came back in full force. Why will you never be a healer? Because self-hatred, locked up in those ridiculous images that you keep revisiting every day as an excuse, reinforces the illness of today. We can never heal such a person unless we decapitate them. Then we heal them. Or we perform a spiritual lobotomy and then it is done.

What are we trying to cut out? The incessant need to blame oneself for some stupid love affair gone sour, and that is all sickness is. The past is throwing it to the present and the body is where it gets it. We can never heal you. I don't care how many lords, blue beings, bright lights, and UFOs come in, they will never do the job because, first off, you refuse to have it happen. You say, "Well, that is not true. I am so tired of feeling this way." Then stop going backwards.

Now here is the twist to that. That also means that when we discharge the past finally and no longer refer to it, we no longer manifest it. So what happens is the wellness starts to come because the generation of sickness that is stimulated by the mind no longer has the stimulating going on, so therefore there is a wellness that starts to come and a centeredness of well-beingness. That is the gift of one who is pure in Spirit, pure in mind. You won't ever get sick again because the reason for being sick is no longer there.

Most of you who suffer are at the hands of your own undoing because you always go backward. In your moments of the most severe pain, you think about your condition constantly, which of course now it is too late because it is there on you. It is best to curb this while you can. Your eyesight will improve, your hearing will improve, your stamina will return, your appetite will normalize itself, your skin will look better, because your hormones are flowing equally. All of the centers in the body are working on the same level with the same energy. The energy can now move through every single one of them without an apparition or a destruction, without the shadow. All seven centers are connected with glands and when the energy is moving through all of those centers, all of those glands, including the thalamus, are all discharging hormones, harmony. Then we have wellness, total wellness.

Manifestation then in the present is the only way, the godly way, that it comes. When you are that clear, my beautiful people, when I tell you to do something you won't have a second thought. You know what the second thought is? Referencing backwards. It is simple to understand what that means. Just think the thoughts that you think when I tell you to do something. Be aware of what you are thinking and you will catch yourself. You are referencing backwards. The moment I tell you to focus on fabulous wealth, you know what is your reference? Resentment and lack. It isn't simply a surrender into the teaching. It isn't simply an ultimate surrender into the discipline. You don't even surrender. You walk backwards to reference it. So you have walked to the past. You have left my august body, you have walked backwards, you have lived in lack, and so you move through the discipline from the past, not the present. If you are in the present you become it immediately, and when you do, the light of the Holy Spirit shines and your God radiates through you. Your brain is turned on to create the thought-form and then you move into it — that becomes the present-Now — and when you do, there are no shadows. There is no way the light and the energy can be splintered to hold up the phantoms of yesterday. It has a clear path of entry. Then it becomes. That is what is meant by the purity of Spirit.

What are the advantages to finding your resentment and your lack? So that you can get rid of them, you can find honesty in yourself. When you are honest in yourself, you can sleep at night. When you are honest with yourself, you have joy in the moment. You are not having to be clever. You are not having to be diplomatic. You are not having to tell lies. You are being clear. The clearer you are, the brighter your radiance is going to shine because you have dispensed with it. Nobody is worth being cloudy for, no one is, and no incident in your life is worth being "fogged" for.

Now that is what a true master must do, so therefore now you understand what it is to lay it on the altar. It is painful the moment you start doing it, and in the next moment you have joy because it is as if somebody has relieved a burden off your shoulders. They have. You have done it. What you did was let your little self run to the present, finally, and you cut all the ropes to the past. This is not hard to do in practicality, not if your supreme goal is to be the Lord God of your being. And what could have been pales to what will be. So what little thought-form went through your head then? Did you run backwards, think about all the wealth you had and compare it to what will be? If you can do this with clarity, and what you can have is unlimited, did that put a smile on your face?

What about that lover you left behind? There will come a day they will pass in front of you and they will look like an old crow. I don't care how young they are, they will look old. You know why? Because they are part of what you cut out and they are still living back there. They don't have radiant energy, that is for sure, and it shows. Always say to these people, "You wear your past very well." They are exercising eight hours a day to generate health, so they always have that winced look in their face. Ever seen a smiling, happy runner? I never did. They are suffering. They don't have the vital energy. They wheeze and are old. They are back there in the past. And when you look at them, they have no color in their face, there is no light in those eyes, there is a fit body but it is not well. We know it is not well because it doesn't have vital energy. So the energy of the day is being thrown into the body to beef it up. They look old, they are not well, and they are locked into the trauma of their past. Why in the world would you want to court disaster? Why would you want to do that? Never, never.

Then you will find beings of equal substance, and they will be the light of your life because they are what you are. Their radiance and their beauty are perpetual. They have a song in their heart and a light in their eyes. They are equal to who you are. They stand in the present with you. Isn't that beautiful? They compare you to no one, no one but what they are. How beautiful that is. That is my God.

When you are unencumbered by that which is termed the ghosts of yesterday, the haunts of yesterday, the what-ifs of yesterday, it means you became honest with yourself. Thank God. When you are unencumbered by them you don't lack for anything because you are so clear that when the desire comes, the need is met. And it is so sweet. Masters don't have surprises. They make them. Do you find it simple? And why is that? Because I said so, but that is the truth. I said so and you heard it, and you said so too. So be it.

People get a little confused about what change is. They think if they move from one place to another, that is change, but in order to do this you must change it first in thought. If you are going to leave the past, you must leave it first completely in your mind, consciously leave it. Then you pursue the absence, followed with the body. Whatsoever you think, you might as well have already done because to me if you have the thought, you have done the deed. You cannot be hypocritical to the teachings that consciousness and energy creates reality. No one in this room should misunderstand that what you think is the ground of all being. It is. Thoughts are real. They are the only reality, and what follows is a mirror of them in the form of energy. It is the thought that holds the seed of true reality, and energy emulates it through form.

So now what you think in your brain is really who you are. It is not where you are. It is who you are in your head. To make any change, that is where it must come, and there the Great Work must be done. You must know that your thoughts are things and that you are known by them. Those are your deeds, not what you do with your hands but what you do with your mind. That is how you are weighed in the end. So first we must leave the past through thought and we must have closure. We must close the door and walk away from it. When we insist every day to refer only to this present moment, "I am what I am now" — not "I am what I am because of what happened to me in my juvenile years" — then there is nothing to weigh me by but who I am this moment.

Every day should be that present moment and when it is, you will be filled with incredible joy. To your sheer delight the smallest of things that you wonder and ponder will manifest, and the wonderful things that you desire will just happen to you because there is nothing standing in the way. You are here in the present, you wanted them in the present, and the present is where they can find you. They are not going to find you in the past. Your present desire here can never manifest ten years ago. What you want cannot manifest in a mind that is still caught ten years ago because the manifestation doesn't belong ten years ago. It belongs now.

Health can only be delivered to the recipient in the present. Health cannot be delivered to you five years ago. If you are caught in the path of five years ago with the same thinking, health will never find you there because it was never meant to be a part of your past. It is only a part of the present.

The loaf of bread that you want in your hand, that loaf of bread that you manifest will not find you two hours earlier when you were starving. If you are still starving like you were two hours earlier, you are living in the past and the bread will not find you. It can only find you in the moment.

The joy that you want was not a part of your past so how can you expect to get it yesterday? Don't you understand how the mechanics of consciousness works? Joy was never meant for yesterday. It was meant for now. The recipient has to stand right here in that moment without any prints backwards to receive what is desired now. You see, we get everything always. We wear the crown of kings and queens, we carry the great swords of conquerors, but the problem with us is that we are always leaving them behind for lesser things. Where the glory of God should always be manifesting, we are never there to receive it.

Learning How to Defy Time:
The Mind of the True Master

Stop thinking that it is about linear time. It is not. Stop thinking that this means literally that you have moved in with your old husbandman or old wife. That is not what I am saying. I am telling you that the only reality is thought, and if you are already there, if that is where your thinking is, you are in the past. Your body may be here at half past five but your consciousness is fourteen years ago, so the bounty that we want now we only get if we are Now. No one can stand in for us. We cannot send a substitute. We cannot send a guide or an angel or a teacher. We cannot send our friend, our neighbor, our lover. It is we who must stand in the moment to receive what it is we have asked for.

It is what we think. You could be fifty or a hundred and fifty years old with an old brain and worn-out energy, but you are still stuck at twenty with the traumas at twenty. Do you know why, stuck at twenty, you still aged? Because you stayed in the past. Holding the present is where we defy time. We defy it.

You are going to find that you are going to say, "My God, the sacrifice is too big to give up my past, to give up my altered ego, my arrogance, my ignorance, my jealousy, my limitations, my suffering, my whining nature, my envy, my thievery, my dishonesty, my cleverness, my art of manifestation on how to delude people. I have become a master at it. You are asking a great deal of me to give that up." Yes, I am, but when you do that is when we say you are now purified, you are now pure in Spirit. To your sheer amazement you will be analogical, and the gift of what you are focusing on you will finally be in the place to receive it.

Where is the place you need to work the most? You have to leave the past first, consciously, and then when you are ready you leave it physically. You have to, and with no regrets.

So then this is the key. Why is it I can revisit my past so often when I am with you? Because I don't regret any of my past, and I loved it. It was colorful, it was not boring, it was challenging, it was passionate, it was powerful, and I conquered and I knew. Have I ever regretted laying down Onai? Hell, no, I don't. I don't do that. Did I ever rebuild it in my mind? No. I like it the way I did it.

A master becomes aware of every thought and looks in no direction that would prompt him to think other than his wishes. You remember that. That is such a clear and wonderful statement about the past: Don't look backwards and don't look at people, places, things, times, and events. Now you begin to understand what was so marvelous about that teaching. Focus on this without people, places, times, and events, and what do you have? The Now.

What could I have possibly left out of the picture? I have left nothing out of it: people, places, things, times, and events. You don't look backwards. You don't drag them into the picture. You just stay present, utterly and totally. You don't want to go back there and patch up anything. Let the wounds bleed. Let them bleed. Don't go back and say "I am sorry." I never said I was sorry. I never sent an envoy my deepest apologies, because I wasn't. Why would I say I am sorry when I really wasn't, because it would make me look better? Who was I looking better for? No one.

I was never sorry about anything I did. That is why I was an honest man. That is a far cry from what you are. And I never apologized for my actions. My actions were what I was. What do I apologize for hacking someone's head off when they are born thirty years later? "I am sorry I hacked your head off so you can have this wonderful life now." Why should we apologize for that? There is no logic and reason in it. It seems arrogant and brutal. I was all of those things. I was an honest man. That is why I was powerful and that is why I was fearless.

When you are honest, you don't have any fear. Have you ever thought about that? When you are an honorable person and you are pure in Spirit, there is no such thing as fear, because what would that be? We are only afraid of what we have created. You know the axiom, "Do unto others as you would have them do unto you"? If you have been mean to other people, if you have lied about other people, if you have started rumors about other people, if you have abused them, if you have used them, if you have stolen from them, if you have been adulterous with them, if you have been all of those things, you have a lot of reason to be afraid because you have created the circumstances of your own fear.

You see, when you are a master, there aren't any surprises. We know that what we do, we are. When you are an honorable man and there are no regrets, there is no fear. And what does an honorable man do? None of those things. You can be a conqueror and not be a heinous creature of mediocrity. There is honor in conquest. That is why you are worried and that is why you can't sleep at night and that is why you are fighting your age with everything that you have because what you are is coming on strong right back to you. Don't you understand that there are no accidents in nature and there are certainly none in consciousness. You will never lose what you have never taken.

So now we get a little more honed in, if you will, on what this beautiful entity that I say you are really is and that perhaps, somewhere inside of you, you wish to be. You begin to see it is not really a fanatic and it is not really someone that has swung into the world of ne'er-do-wellness. It is not someone who is out there in outer space or someone who is talking nonsense. It is not about someone who sits out in the back field or on their own property or someone else's property with their hands held out thinking that it is owed to them, that they don't have to do anything but leech off of other people. You see, that is not spiritual.

It isn't about what you eat. You need to know what you eat, because you are excessive in everything. When you become more of a present person, there will not be any excesses. There just won't be. There will be an evenness with everything and nothing will be bad.

We begin to see that then the nature of masters takes on this whole different form than that angelic form you thought that we had. Remember I warned you, you may not even notice one of us. We have ears missing and scars across our face. I liked my scars. I didn't have them cosmetically removed or spiritually circumcised. I liked the color of my skin. I thought it was beautiful. I liked the color of my hair. I thought it was beautiful. I like the color of my eyes. I think they are beautiful. I like my nose, my jaw, my long gait, and my height very much but, you see, that is how we all are. You would never really notice us except that we look a little different in the crowd because we are a little bit bigger than most people. And then, of course, there are the dwarves of five-foot-seven. We are a strange company.

We are not all that polished stuff that you think we are. We love all that we were. We labored in the fields of life to love ourselves, and we deserve ourselves. We wear the scars of our journey. They are beautiful. The scar my love made across my face I wore till the day I left this plane and then beyond. The sword in my back and through my belly I still have in all of my bodies. I like it. It was my baptism. Why should I not keep it?

We are beginning to see now that the nature of what we want to be is so different than our delusion of what we thought it was. That was only the delusion of an altered ego that really sort of dehumanized you, didn't it, because it made all the angels with golden hair and golden skin and azure-blue eyes. It dehumanized you. It made you less than something that is celestial. I want you to know you are beautiful. What we really look like are you, who just stopped aging, because we found the present and cut the chains of the past. And that makes you closer to us, not farther from us.

This woman is a master — you would never know it — cleverly disguised. That is how we all are. That is the good news for you because it means you are closer than you ever thought before, and you don't have to have long golden locks or long ebony locks or copper-haired beauty. You don't have to be beautiful at all. Your God's light is beautiful. That is intoxicating. That will take the plainest of faces and the sloppiest of bodies and will mold them to an unearthly beauty because it is the soul. It is the body of the Holy Spirit. We are a motley company but we are all beautiful.

You begin to see what we are. You begin to see how we think, and maybe it is not that we think at all but that we are really creators. You begin to understand how we are so detached from you and yet we bring you close to us. We don't move closer to you. You come close to us because we are detached from all that you stand for. We are detached from your pain and your suffering and your need to reclaim that victory every day of your life. We have already done that. So soon those of you who pass this way must do that as well.

You begin to see that we are not fanatics, that we were rightly chosen all along. We just knew how to live. You don't. That is what I am teaching you to do because it has been a great effort to teach one thing and then have your imagination run off with it and see it in delusionary form and then swing you back over this way so that you see it a little more real and bombastic. I am trying to get you to the middle.

You don't have to do anything but stop living in yesterday and hear me when I talk to you, hear me with all your might so that every word I say resonates in your brain and creates the thought-form the teacher wants to give you. The words are a gift because they make you form the picture of the word, which is responsible for creating reality. There is no one going to tell you what I have told you.

When you listen, you get closer. You start to think. If you were hearing every word I was saying, then your brain for the first time was actually operating the way a master's brain operates just because I was making you listen to me and you were having to hear the words. The brain has to form the pictures of the words in order for us to define hearing, and understanding means that the pictures are happening. I forced you to think like me.

So you got a little closer to the skin of what I am and what we are that live in this great spiritual environment. You begin to see how we think because I made you think that way, and it wasn't over your head. I daresay that I took this knowledge very nicely and carved it right down to your acceptability. I allowed you to understand. Then when you did, you were present with me. I tell you, while you were present with me you didn't feel any pain, you didn't have any emotional hurt, you didn't feel any lack, you didn't feel any time. You were just me. That is a master teacher. And that, master students, is how you are supposed to feel all of the time. When you are in this moment, that is the reward of it because there is no yesterday so there is no pain, there is no suffering, there is no agony, there is no envy, there is no want, there is no desire. There is only this moment, and it is everything.

So we went from telling you you haven't done the work, and you haven't. You have done very little to make the day a masterful day. We took you from where you were to thinking just like a master. And if you can do that every day — because, my God, now why wouldn't you want to? — if you can do that every day and every moment, then you are thinking like I am thinking. Then with that you have brought about, first, spiritual presence. Remember this little story I told you here about how God is always manifesting your fabulous wealth, your healing, everything, but you are not present to receive it? That presence creates the reality that allows what you have never seen to become in full view. Then you can engage the masters because you can be present.

The masters are always here. I am always here.

I love you. So be it.

— *Ramtha*

RAMTHA'S GLOSSARY

Analogical. Being analogical means living in the Now. It is the creative moment and is outside of time, the past, and the emotions.

Analogical mind. Analogical mind means one mind. It is the result of the alignment of primary consciousness and secondary consciousness, the Observer and the personality. The fourth, fifth, sixth, and seventh seals of the body are opened in this state of mind. The bands spin in opposite directions, like a wheel within a wheel, creating a powerful vortex that allows the thoughts held in the frontal lobe to coagulate and manifest.

Bands, the. The bands are the two sets of seven frequencies that surround the human body and hold it together. Each of the seven frequency layers of each band corresponds to the seven seals of seven levels of consciousness in the human body. The bands are the auric field that allow the processes of binary and analogical mind.

Binary mind. This term means two minds. It is the mind produced by accessing the knowledge of the human personality and the physical body without accessing our deep subconscious mind. Binary mind relies solely on the knowledge, perception, and thought processes of the neocortex and the first three seals. The fourth, fifth, sixth, and seventh seals remain closed in this state of mind.

Blue Body®. It is the body that belongs to the fourth plane of existence, the bridge consciousness, and the ultraviolet frequency band. The Blue Body® is the lord over the lightbody and the physical plane.

Blue Body® Dance. It is a discipline taught by Ramtha in which the students lift their conscious awareness to the consciousness of the fourth plane. This discipline allows the Blue Body® to be accessed and the fourth seal to be opened.

Blue Body® Healing. It is a discipline taught by Ramtha in which the students lift their conscious awareness to the consciousness of the fourth plane and the Blue Body® for the purpose of healing or changing the physical body.

Blue webs. The blue webs represent the basic structure at a subtle level of the physical body. It is the invisible skeletal structure of the physical realm vibrating at the level of ultraviolet frequency.

Body/mind consciousness. Body/mind consciousness is the consciousness that belongs to the physical plane and the human body.

Book of Life. Ramtha refers to the soul as the Book of Life, where the whole journey of involution and evolution of each individual is recorded in the form of wisdom.

C&E® = R. Consciousness and energy create the nature of reality.

C&E®. Abbreviation of Consciousness & Energy^{SM}. This is the service mark of the fundamental discipline of manifestation and the raising of consciousness taught in Ramtha's School of Enlightenment. Through this discipline the students learn to create an analogical state of mind, open up their higher seals, and create reality from the Void. A Beginning C&E® Workshop is the name of the Introductory Workshop for beginning students in which they learn the fundamental concepts and disciplines of Ramtha's teachings. The teachings of the Beginning C&E® Workshop can be found in *Ramtha, A Beginner's Guide to Creating Reality,* third ed. (Yelm: JZK Publishing, a division of JZK, Inc., 2004), and in *Ramtha, Creating Personal Reality*, Tape 380 ed. (Yelm: Ramtha Dialogues, 1998).

Christwalk. The Christwalk is a discipline designed by Ramtha in which the student learns to walk very slowly being acutely aware. In this discipline the students learn to manifest, with each step they take, the mind of a Christ.

Consciousness. Consciousness is the child who was born from the Void's contemplation of itself. It is the essence and fabric of all being. Everything that exists originated in consciousness and manifested outwardly through its handmaiden energy. A stream of consciousness refers to the continuum of the mind of God.

Consciousness and energy. Consciousness and energy are the dynamic force of creation and are inextricably combined. Everything that exists originated in consciousness and manifested through the modulation of its energy impact into mass.

Create Your Day^{SM}. This is the service mark for a technique created by Ramtha for raising consciousness and energy and intentionally creating a constructive plan of experiences and events for the day early in the morning before the start of the day. This technique is exclusively taught at Ramtha's School of Enlightenment.

Disciplines of the Great Work. Ramtha's School of Ancient Wisdom is dedicated to the Great Work. The disciplines of the Great Work practiced in Ramtha's School of Enlightenment are all designed in their entirety by Ramtha. These practices are powerful initiations where the student has the opportunity to apply and experience firsthand the teachings of Ramtha.

Emotional body. The emotional body is the collection of past emotions, attitudes, and electrochemical patterns that make up the brain's neuronet and define the human personality of an individual. Ramtha describes it as the seduction of the unenlightened. It is the reason for cyclical reincarnation.

Emotions. An emotion is the physical, biochemical effect of an experience. Emotions belong to the past, for they are the expression of experiences that are already known and mapped in the neuropathways of the brain.

Energy. Energy is the counterpart of consciousness. All consciousness carries with it a dynamic energy impact, radiation, or natural expression of itself. Likewise, all forms of energy carry with it a consciousness that defines it.

Enlightenment. Enlightenment is the full realization of the human person, the attainment of immortality, and unlimited mind. It is the result of raising the kundalini energy sitting at the base of the spine to the seventh seal that opens the dormant parts of the brain. When the energy penetrates the lower cerebellum and the midbrain, and the subconscious mind is opened, the individual experiences a blinding flash of light called enlightenment.

Evolution. Evolution is the journey back home from the slowest levels of frequency and mass to the highest levels of consciousness and Point Zero.

Fieldwork^{SM}. Fieldwork^{SM} is one of the fundamental disciplines of Ramtha's School of Enlightenment. The students are taught to create a symbol of something they want to know and experience and draw it on a paper card. These cards are placed with the blank side facing out on the fence rails of a large field. The students blindfold themselves and focus on their symbol, allowing their body to walk freely to find their card through the application of the law of consciousness and energy and analogical mind.

Fifth plane. The fifth plane of existence is the plane of superconsciousness and x-ray frequency. It is also known as the Golden Plane or paradise.

Fifth seal. This seal is the center of our spiritual body that connects us to the fifth plane. It is associated with the thyroid gland and with speaking and living the truth without dualism.

First plane. It refers to the material or physical plane. It is the plane of the image consciousness and Hertzian frequency. It is the slowest and densest form of coagulated consciousness and energy.

First seal. The first seal is associated with the reproductive organs, sexuality, and survival.

First three seals. The first three seals are the seals of sexuality, pain and suffering, and controlling power. These are the seals commonly at play in all of the complexities of the human drama.

Fourth plane. The fourth plane of existence is the realm of the bridge consciousness and ultraviolet frequency. This plane is described as the plane of Shiva, the destroyer of the old and creator of the new. In this plane, energy is not yet split into positive and negative polarity. Any lasting changes or healing of the physical body must be changed first at the level of the fourth plane and the Blue Body®. This plane is also called the Blue Plane, or the plane of Shiva.

Fourth seal. The fourth seal is associated with unconditional love and the thymus gland. When this seal is activated, a hormone is released that maintains the body in perfect health and stops the aging process.

God. Ramtha's teachings are an exposition of the statement, "You are God." Humanity is described as the forgotten Gods, divine beings by nature who have forgotten their heritage and true identity. It is precisely this statement that represents Ramtha's challenging message to our modern age, an age riddled with religious superstition and misconceptions about the divine and the true knowledge of wisdom.

God within. It is the Observer, the great self, the primary consciousness, the Spirit, the God within the human person.

God/man. The full realization of a human being.

God/woman. The full realization of a human being.

Gods. The Gods are technologically advanced beings from other star systems who came to Earth 455,000 years ago. These Gods manipulated the human race genetically, mixing and modifying our DNA with theirs. They are responsible for the evolution of the neocortex and used the human race as a subdued work force. Evidence of these events is recorded in the Sumerian tablets and artifacts. This term is also used to describe the true identity of humanity, the forgotten Gods.

Golden body. It is the body that belongs to the fifth plane, superconsciousness, and x-ray frequency.

Great Work. The Great Work is the practical application of the knowledge of the Schools of Ancient Wisdom. It refers to the disciplines by which the human person becomes enlightened and is transmuted into an immortal, divine being.

Grid^{SM}, The. This is the service mark for a technique created by Ramtha for raising consciousness and energy and intentionally tapping into the Zero Point Energy field and the fabric of reality through a mental visualization. This technique is exclusively taught at Ramtha's School of Enlightenment.

Hierophant. A hierophant is a master teacher who is able to manifest what they teach and initiate their students into such knowledge.

Hyperconsciousness. Hyperconsciousness is the consciousness of the sixth plane and gamma ray frequency.

Infinite Unknown. It is the frequency band of the seventh plane of existence and ultraconsciousness.

Involution. Involution is the journey from Point Zero and the seventh plane to the slowest and densest levels of frequency and mass.

JZ Knight. JZ Knight is the only person appointed by Ramtha to channel him. Ramtha refers to JZ as his beloved daughter. She was Ramaya, the eldest of the children given to Ramtha during his lifetime.

Kundalini. Kundalini energy is the life force of a person that descends from the higher seals to the base of the spine at puberty. It is a large packet of energy reserved for human evolution, commonly pictured as a coiled serpent that sits at the base of the spine. This energy is different from the energy coming out of the first three seals responsible for sexuality, pain and suffering, power, and victimization. It is commonly described as the sleeping serpent or the sleeping dragon. The journey of the kundalini energy to the crown of the head is called the journey of enlightenment. This journey takes place when this serpent wakes up and starts to split and dance around the spine, ionizing the spinal fluid and changing its molecular structure. This action causes the opening of the midbrain and the door to the subconscious mind.

Life force. The life force is the Father/Mother, the Spirit, the breath of life within the person that is the platform from which the person creates its illusions, imagination, and dreams.

Life review. It is the review of the previous incarnation that occurs when the person reaches the third plane after death. The person gets the opportunity to be the Observer, the actor, and the recipient of its own actions. The unresolved issues from that lifetime that emerge at the life or light review set the agenda for the next incarnation.

Light, the. The light refers to the third plane of existence.

Lightbody. It is the same as the radiant body. It is the body that belongs to the third plane of conscious awareness and the visible light frequency band.

List, the. The List is the discipline taught by Ramtha where the student gets to write a list of items they desire to know and experience and then learn to focus on it in an analogical state of consciousness. The List is the map used to design, change, and reprogram the neuronet of the person. It is the tool that helps to bring meaningful and lasting changes in the person and their reality.

Make known the unknown. This phrase expresses the original divine mandate given to the Source consciousness to manifest and bring to conscious awareness all of the infinite potentials of the Void. This statement represents the basic intent that inspires the dynamic process of creation and evolution.

Mind. Mind is the product of streams of consciousness and energy acting on the brain creating thought-forms, holographic segments, or neurosynaptic patterns called memory. The streams of consciousness and energy are what keep the brain alive. They are its power source. A person's ability to think is what gives them a mind.

Mind of God. The mind of God comprises the mind and wisdom of every lifeform that ever lived on any dimension, in any time, or that ever will live on any planet, any star, or region of space.

Mirror consciousness. When Point Zero imitated the act of contemplation of the Void it created a mirror reflection of itself, a point of reference that made the exploration of the Void possible. It is called mirror consciousness or secondary consciousness. See **Self.**

Monkey-mind. Monkey-mind refers to the flickering, swinging mind of the personality.

Mother/Father Principle. It is the source of all life, the Father, the eternal Mother, the Void. In Ramtha's teachings, the Source and God the creator are not the same. God the creator is seen as Point Zero and primary consciousness but not as the Source, or the Void, itself.

Name-field. The name-field is the name of the large field where the discipline of Fieldwork^SM is practiced.

Neighborhood Walk^SM. This is the service mark of a technique created by JZ Knight for raising consciousness and energy and intentionally modifying our neuronets and set patterns of thinking no longer wanted and replacing them with new ones of our choice. This technique is exclusively taught at Ramtha's School of Enlightenment.

Neuronet. The contraction for "neural network," a network of neurons that perform a function together.

Observer. It refers to the Observer responsible for collapsing the particle/wave of quantum mechanics. It represents the great self, the Spirit, primary consciousness, the God within the human person.

Outrageous. Ramtha uses this word in a positive way to express something or someone who is extraordinary and unusual, unrestrained in action, and excessively bold or fierce.

People, places, things, times, and events. These are the main areas of human experience to which the personality is emotionally attached. These areas represent the past of the human person and constitute the content of the emotional body.

Personality, the. See **Emotional body.**

Plane of Bliss. It refers to the plane of rest where souls get to plan their next incarnations after their life reviews. It is also known as heaven and paradise where there is no suffering, no pain, no need or lack, and where every wish is immediately manifested.

Plane of demonstration. The physical plane is also called the plane of demonstration. It is the plane where the person has the opportunity to demonstrate its creative potentiality in mass and witness consciousness in material form in order to expand its emotional understanding.

Point Zero. It refers to the original point of awareness created by the Void through its act of contemplating itself. Point Zero is the original child of the Void, the birth of consciousness.

Primary consciousness. It is the Observer, the great self, the God within the human person.

Ram. Ram is a shorter version of the name Ramtha. Ramtha means the Father.

Ramaya. Ramtha refers to JZ Knight as his beloved daughter. She was Ramaya, the first one to become Ramtha's adopted child during his lifetime. Ramtha found Ramaya abandoned on the steppes of Russia. Many people gave their children to Ramtha during the march as a gesture of love and highest respect; these children were to be raised in the House of the Ram. His children grew to the great number of 133 even though he never had offspring of his own blood.

Ramtha (etymology). The name of Ramtha the Enlightened One, Lord of the Wind, means the Father. It also refers to the Ram who descended from the mountain on what is known as the terrible day of the Ram. "It is about that in all antiquity. And in ancient Egypt, there is an avenue dedicated to the Ram, the great conqueror. And they were wise enough to understand that whoever could walk down the avenue of the Ram could conquer the wind." The word Aram, the name of Noah's grandson, is formed from the Aramaic noun Araa — meaning earth, landmass — and the word Ramtha, meaning high. This Semitic name echoes Ramtha's descent from the high mountain, which began the great march.

Runner. A runner in Ramtha's lifetime was responsible for bringing specific messages or information. A master teacher has the ability to send runners to other people that manifest their words or intent in the form of an experience or an event.

Second plane. It is the plane of existence of social consciousness and the infrared frequency band. It is associated with pain and suffering. This plane is the negative polarity of the third plane of visible light frequency.

Second seal. This seal is the energy center of social consciousness and the infrared frequency band. It is associated with the experience of pain and suffering and is located in the lower abdominal area.

Secondary consciousness. When Point Zero imitated the act of contemplation of the Void it created a mirror reflection of itself, a point of reference that made the exploration of the Void possible. It is called mirror consciousness or secondary consciousness. See **Self.**

Self, the. The self is the true identity of the human person different from the personality. It is the transcendental aspect of the person. It refers to the secondary consciousness, the traveler in a journey of involution and evolution making known the unknown.

Sending-and-receiving. Sending-and-receiving is the name of the discipline taught by Ramtha in which the student learns to access information using the faculties of the midbrain to the exclusion of sensory perception. This discipline develops the student's psychic ability of telepathy and divination.

Seven seals. The seven seals are powerful energy centers that constitute seven levels of consciousness in the human body. The bands are the way in which the physical body is held together according to these seals. In every human being there is energy spiraling out of the first three seals or centers. The energy pulsating out of the first three seals manifests itself respectively as sexuality, pain, or power. When the upper seals are unlocked, a higher level of awareness is activated.

Seventh plane. The seventh plane is the plane of ultraconsciousness and the Infinite Unknown frequency band. This plane is where the journey of involution began. This plane was created by Point Zero when it imitated the act of contemplation of the Void and the mirror or secondary consciousness was created. A plane of existence or dimension of space and time exists between two points of consciousness. All the other planes were created by slowing down the time and frequency band of the seventh plane.

Seventh seal. This seal is associated with the crown of the head, the pituitary gland, and the attainment of enlightenment.

Shiva. The Lord God Shiva represents the Lord of the Blue Plane and the Blue Body®. Shiva is not used in reference to a singular deity from Hinduism. It is rather the representation of a state of consciousness that belongs to the fourth plane, the ultraviolet frequency band, and the opening of the fourth seal. Shiva is neither male nor female. It is an androgynous being, for the energy of the fourth plane has not yet been split into positive and negative polarity. This is an important distinction from the traditional Hindu representation of Shiva as a male deity who has a wife. The tiger skin at its feet, the trident staff, and the sun and the moon at the level of the head represent the mastery of this body over the first three seals of consciousness. The kundalini energy is pictured as fiery energy shooting from the base of the spine through the head. This is another distinction from some Hindu representations of Shiva with the serpent energy coming out at the level of the fifth seal or throat. Another symbolic image of Shiva is the long threads of dark hair and an abundance of pearl necklaces, which represent its richness of experience owned into wisdom. The quiver and bow and arrows are the agent by which Shiva shoots its powerful will and destroys imperfection and creates the new.

Sixth plane. The sixth plane is the realm of hyperconsciousness and the gamma ray frequency band. In this plane the awareness of being one with the whole of life is experienced.

Sixth seal. This seal is associated with the pineal gland and the gamma ray frequency band. The reticular formation that filters and veils the knowingness of the subconscious mind is opened when this seal is activated. The opening of the brain refers to the opening of this seal and the activation of its consciousness and energy.

Social consciousness. It is the consciousness of the second plane and the infrared frequency band. It is also called the image of the human personality and the mind of the first three seals. Social consciousness refers to the collective consciousness of human society. It is the collection of thoughts, assumptions, judgments, prejudices, laws, morality, values, attitudes, ideals, and emotions of the fraternity of the human race.

Soul. Ramtha refers to the soul as the Book of Life, where the whole journey of involution and evolution of the individual is recorded in the form of wisdom.

Subconscious mind. The seat of the subconscious mind is the lower cerebellum or reptilian brain. This part of the brain has its own independent connections to the frontal lobe and the whole of the body and has the power to access the mind of God, the wisdom of the ages.

Superconsciousness. This is the consciousness of the fifth plane and the x-ray frequency band.

Tahumo. Tahumo is the discipline taught by Ramtha in which the student learns the ability to master the effects of the natural environment — cold and heat — on the human body.

Tank field. It is the name of the large field with the labyrinth that is used for the discipline of The Tank®.

Tank®, The. It is the name given to the labyrinth used as part of the disciplines of Ramtha's School of Enlightenment. The students are taught to find the entry to this labyrinth blindfolded and move through it focusing on the Void without touching the walls or using the eyes or the senses. The objective of this discipline is to find, blindfolded, the center of the labyrinth or a room designated and representative of the Void.

Third plane. This is the plane of conscious awareness and the visible light frequency band. It is also known as the light plane and the mental plane. When the energy of the Blue Plane is lowered down to this frequency band, it splits into positive and negative polarity. It is at this point that the soul splits into two, giving origin to the phenomenon of soulmates.

Third seal. This seal is the energy center of conscious awareness and the visible light frequency band. It is associated with control, tyranny, victimization, and power. It is located in the region of the solar plexus.

Thought. Thought is different from consciousness. The brain processes a stream of consciousness, modifying it into segments — holographic pictures — of neurological, electrical, and chemical prints called thoughts. Thoughts are the building blocks of mind.

Torsion Process[SM]. This is the service mark of a technique created by Ramtha for raising consciousness and energy and intentionally creating a torsion field using the mind. Through this technique the student learns to build a wormhole in space/time, alter reality, and create dimensional phenomena such as invisibility, levitation, bilocation, teleportation, and others. This technique is exclusively taught at Ramtha's School of Enlightenment.

Twilight®. This term is used to describe the discipline taught by Ramtha in which the students learn to put their bodies in a catatonic state similar to deep sleep, yet retaining their conscious awareness.

Twilight® Visualization Process. It is the process used to practice the discipline of the List or other visualization formats.

Ultraconsciousness. It is the consciousness of the seventh plane and the Infinite Unknown frequency band. It is the consciousness of an ascended master.

Unknown God. The Unknown God was the single God of Ramtha's ancestors, the Lemurians. The Unknown God also represents the forgotten divinity and divine origin of the human person.

Upper four seals. The upper four seals are the fourth, fifth, sixth, and seventh seals.

Void, the. The Void is defined as one vast nothing materially, yet all things potentially. *See* **Mother/Father Principle.**

Yellow brain. The yellow brain is Ramtha's name for the neocortex, the house of analytical and emotional thought. The reason why it is called the yellow brain is because the neocortices were colored yellow in the original two-dimensional, caricature-style drawing Ramtha used for his teaching on the function of the brain and its processes. He explained that the different aspects of the brain in this particular drawing are exaggerated and colorfully highlighted for the sake of study and understanding. This specific drawing became the standard tool used in all the subsequent teachings on the brain.

Yeshua ben Joseph. Ramtha refers to Jesus Christ by the name Yeshua ben Joseph, following the Jewish traditions of that time.

FIG. A: THE SEVEN SEALS:
SEVEN LEVELS OF CONSCIOUSNESS IN THE HUMAN BODY

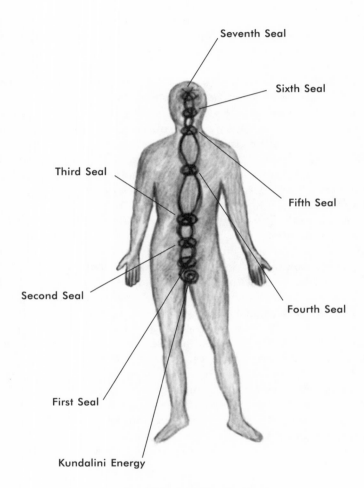

Seventh Seal

Sixth Seal

Third Seal

Fifth Seal

Second Seal

Fourth Seal

First Seal

Kundalini Energy

Ramtha's Glossary

Fig. B: Seven Levels of Consciousness and Energy

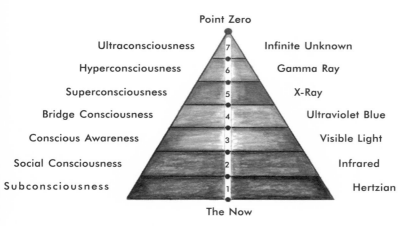

Point Zero

Ultraconsciousness	7	Infinite Unknown
Hyperconsciousness	6	Gamma Ray
Superconsciousness	5	X-Ray
Bridge Consciousness	4	Ultraviolet Blue
Conscious Awareness	3	Visible Light
Social Consciousness	2	Infrared
Subconsciousness	1	Hertzian

The Now

Copyright © 2000 JZ Knight

Fig. C: The Brain

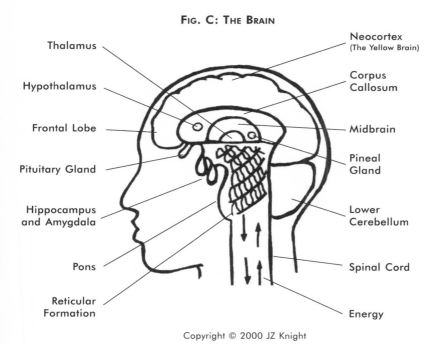

Thalamus
Hypothalamus
Frontal Lobe
Pituitary Gland
Hippocampus and Amygdala
Pons
Reticular Formation

Neocortex (The Yellow Brain)
Corpus Callosum
Midbrain
Pineal Gland
Lower Cerebellum
Spinal Cord
Energy

Copyright © 2000 JZ Knight

93

Fig. D: Binary Mind — Living the Image

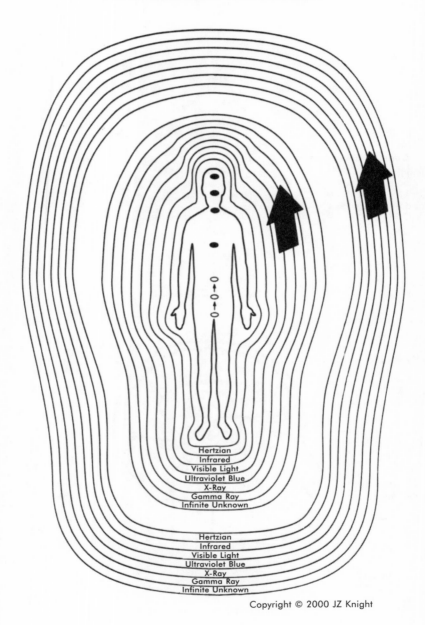

FIG. E: ANALOGICAL MIND — LIVING IN THE NOW

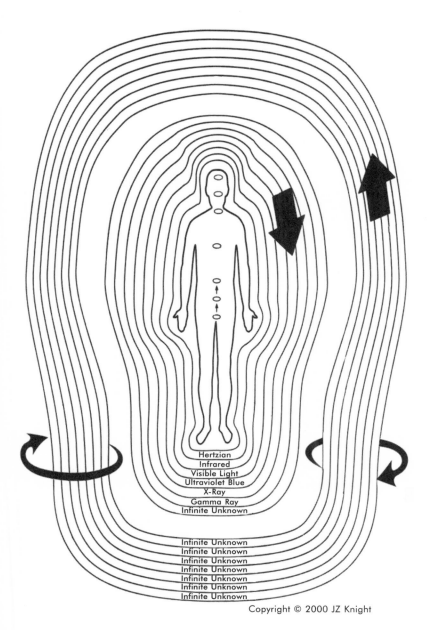

Hertzian
Infrared
Visible Light
Ultraviolet Blue
X-Ray
Gamma Ray
Infinite Unknown

Infinite Unknown
Infinite Unknown
Infinite Unknown
Infinite Unknown
Infinite Unknown
Infinite Unknown
Infinite Unknown

Ramtha's School of Enlightenment
THE SCHOOL OF ANCIENT WISDOM

A Division of JZK, Inc.
P.O. Box 1210
Yelm, Washington 98597
360.458.5201
800.347.0439
www.ramtha.com
www.jzkpublishing.com